국보사진집 百濟金銅大香爐

백제금동대향로

부여扶餘에서 바라보다

Photo Album of National Treasures

Meeting the Gaze of Great Gilt-bronze Incense Burner of Baekje, Buyeo

국립부여박물관
Buyeo National Museum

백제금동대향로
百濟金銅大香爐

백제 百濟
부여 능산리 사지(사적) 扶餘 陵山里 寺址(史蹟)
국보 國寶
부여5333

Great Gilt-bronze Incense Burner of Baekje

Baekje Kingdom
Temple Site in Neungsan-ri, Buyeo(Historic Site)
National Treasure
buyeo5333

부여 부소산 낙화암에서 바라본 백마강(금강)
Baengmagang(Geumgang) River Viewed from Nakhwaam Cliff on Busosan Mountain, Buyeo

발간사

백제금동대향로百濟金銅大香爐 부여扶餘에서 바라보다

백제금동대향로는 1993년 12월 12일, 부여 왕릉원인 능산리 고분군의 서쪽에 위치한 능산리 사지에서 발굴된 이래, 백제 문화를 상징하는 대표적인 문화유산으로 자리매김했습니다. 백제금동대향로의 독보적인 창의성과 예술성은 백제 문화의 정수이자 유래를 찾기 힘든 역사적 가치를 드러냅니다.

백제금동대향로는 1994년 4월 국립중앙박물관의 특별 전시를 시작으로 1996년 5월 30일 국보(당시 제287호) 지정 이후, 1999년 2월부터 현재까지 국립부여박물관에서 상설로 전시되며 사비 백제의 역사와 문화를 변함없이 전해주고 있습니다.

특히 올해 국립부여박물관은 백제금동대향로를 단독으로 전시하는 건축공간인 '백제대향로관'을 개관해 그 가치를 새롭게 보전하고 널리 알리는 이정표를 남기고자 합니다. 이는 1,400여 년 전 백제금동대향로가 세상에 나온 이후 다시 깨어난 30여 년의 시간을 넘어, 미래와 인류를 향한 문화유산으로 그 우수성과 아름다움을 영구히 기리는 첫걸음이라 하겠습니다.

백제금동대향로의 위용을 담은 국보사진집 『백제금동대향로百濟金銅大香爐, 부여扶餘에서 바라보다』는 새로운 전시관 건립을 기념하며 사비 백제의 수도였던 부여에서 마주하는 백제금동대향로의 순간을 담고자, 백제금동대향로의 면모를 감상할 수 있는 사진과 함께 향로 속 자연과 같은 부여의 풍경을 실었습니다.

이 사진집은 백제금동대향로를 품고 그 영원성을 이어가는 부여, 그리고 이곳에서 사비 백제의 맥을 잇는 백제금동대향로의 의미를 사진으로 간직할 수 있는 국보 아카이브가 될 것입니다.

신 영 호
국립부여박물관장

Foreword

Meeting the Gaze of Great Gilt-bronze Incense Burner of Baekje, Buyeo

The Great Gilt-bronze Incense Burner of Baekje, unearthed on December 12, 1993 from the temple site in Neungsan-ri to the west of the Neungsan-ri Ancient Tombs—part of the royal tomb complex in Buyeo—has since come to be regarded as an iconic cultural treasure symbolizing Baekje civilization. Its unparalleled creativity and artistry embody the very essence of Baekje culture, revealing a historical significance and value rarely matched in the ancient world.

Beginning with its special exhibition at the National Museum of Korea in April 1994 and its designation as a National Treasure (then No. 287) on May 30, 1996, the Great Gilt-bronze Incense Burner of Baekje has been on permanent display at the Buyeo National Museum since February 1999. Throughout this time, it has continued to convey the history and culture of Sabi-period Baekje.

This year the Buyeo National Museum opened the Baekje Great Incense Burner Hall, an exhibition space dedicated exclusively to the display of the Great Gilt-bronze Incense Burner of Baekje, marking a new milestone in preserving and sharing its enduring significance. This initiative represents a meaningful first step toward commemorating, in perpetuity, the excellence and beauty of the incense burner—not only as a masterpiece rediscovered some thirty years ago, but as a cultural heritage that will continue to inspire future generations and humanity at large, more than 1,400 years after its creation.

The photo album of national treasures *Meeting the Gaze of Great Gilt-bronze Incense Burner of Baekje, Buyeo* was published to commemorate the opening of the new exhibition gallery. It captures the presence and grandeur of the incense burner as encountered in Buyeo, the former capital of Sabi-period Baekje. The volume pairs detailed photographs that highlight the incense burner's refined features with images of Buyeo's landscapes—evocative of the natural world depicted within the burner itself.

This photo album will serve as a national-treasure archive that preserves, through images, both the legacy of Buyeo—home to the Great Gilt-bronze Incense Burner of Baekje and guardian of its enduring presence—and the significance of the incense burner itself, which carries forward the spirit of Sabi-period Baekje in this very place.

Shin Youngho
Director, Buyeo Natioanal Museum

부여 능산리 사지(사적)
Temple Site in Neungsan-ri, Buyeo(Historic Site)

백제금동대향로百濟金銅大香爐

백제인의 이상향을 펼치다

백제 문화의 정수精髓라고 불리는 백제금동대향로는 1993년 12월 12일, 부여 왕릉원의 서쪽에 주차장 조성을 위한 발굴 조사 중 능산리 절터 공방지의 나무 수조 안에서 그 모습이 드러났다.

향로가 발견된 능산리 절은 목탑터에서 나온 석조사리감(567년, 국보)의 명문으로 미루어, 관산성 전투(554년)에서 전사한 성왕聖王(재위 523~554년)을 기리기 위해 위덕왕威德王(재위 554~598년) 시기에 세워진 왕실의 원찰願刹, 또는 능사陵寺로 이해된다. 발굴 당시 향로 위로 기와 조각과 점토가 차곡차곡 쌓여 있었는데, 660년 사비도성 함락 시점에 향로를 급히 숨기거나 보호하려 했던 것으로 추측되기도 한다.

향로는 전체 높이 62.3cm, 무게 11.8kg으로, 몸체(연꽃과 생명 세계)와 받침(용), 뚜껑(신산神山 세계와 봉황)으로 구성된다. 몸체는 연꽃 형태로 표현되어 고대 문명의 창조 신화와 불교에서 정토·청정의 세계를 상징한다. 연꽃잎 위에는 날개 달린 물고기, 짐승에 올라탄 인물, 물새, 수달 등 수중·지상·공중의 생명들이 공존하며, 받침인 용은 역동적인 자세와 힘찬 기세로 몸체와 뚜껑을 떠받치고 있다.

뚜껑은 도교에서 이상향으로 여겨진 신산을 형상화했다. 꼭대기의 봉황은 턱 아래 구슬을 괸 채 지그시 아래 세상을 내려다보고 있다. 그 밑에는 다섯 명의 연주자가 백제삼현, 종적, 배소, 백제금, 북과 같은 악기로 마치 천상의 음악을 연주하듯이 정교하게 표현되어 있다. 굽이치는 산악, 인물과 동물, 상상 속 영수靈獸들이 능숙한 조형감으로 배치되어, 이상향을 누비는 생명들의 서사를 구성하고 있다. 향의 연기가 피어오를 때 이 조형적 세계는 실제로 살아 움직이는 듯한 감각적 효과를 낸다.

백제금동대향로는 중국 한대漢代 박산향로의 전통을 따르면서 백제 특유의 조형 감각과 종교적 세계관이 결합한 창의적 재구성이 특징이다. 봉황, 산악 등의 요소는 남북조 문화의 영향과 관련된 한편, 코끼리·원숭이와 같은 남방 지역의 동물은 백제가 동남아 지역과 교류가 있었음을 시사한다. 또한 향로의 도상들은 도교적 신선 사상과 토착 신앙, 그리고 사회 전반에 확산한 불교 신앙이 융합되어 백제 사회의 정신세계를 반영한다.

백제금동대향로는 단순한 의기儀器가 아니라 고대국가 백제의 왕권 개념, 종교적 이상세계, 조형미의 절정이 응축된 작품으로, 동아시아 고대 금속공예의 정점이자 백제 문화의 상징적인 걸작으로 평가할 수 있다.

연꽃, 신산, 그리고 봉황

Lotus-shaped Body, Mountain-shaped Lid, and *Bonghwang* at the Summit

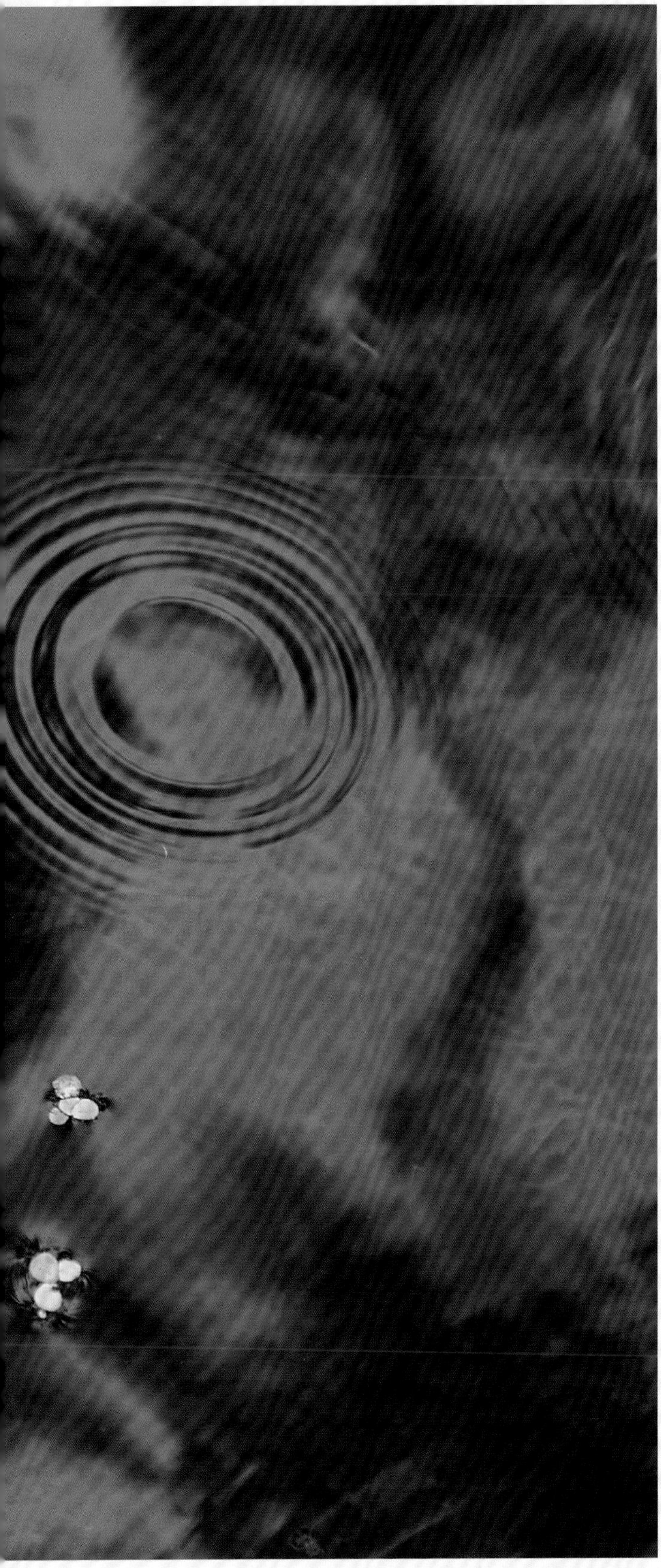

부여 궁남지 연못

Gungnamji Pond, Buyeo, with Floating Lotus Leaves

연꽃을 받친 용

Dragon-shaped Pedestal

부여 궁남지 연꽃

Lotus Blossoms at Gungnamji Pond, Buyeo

연꽃을 닮은 향로
Lotus-shaped Body of the Incense Burner

부여 궁남지(사적)

Gungnamji Pond, Buyeo(Historic Site)

연꽃과 신산 사이, 굽이치는 경계
Bands with Incised Design between Body and Lid

부여 부소산과 백마강(금강)
Busosan Mountain and Baengmagang(Geumgang) River, Buyeo

봉황이 굽어보는 신산

Mountain-shaped Lid Overlooked by *Bonghwang*

향연이 오르는 길, 신산과 봉황의 열두 구멍

Ten Apertures on the Mountain-shaped Lid and Two on *Bongwhang*

부여 백마강(금강) 강변
Riverbank of the Baengmagang(Geumgang) River, Buyeo

인물과 동물이 어우러진 신산
Mountain-shaped Lid with Figures and Animals

부여 금성산 소나무숲

Pine Forest on Geumseongsan Mountain, Buyeo

부여 자온대

Jaondae Rock, Buyeo

다섯 명의 연주자, 그 곁의 새 다섯
Five Musicians, with Five Birds Nearby

부여 능산리 사지(사적)
Temple Site in Neungsan-ri, Buyeo(Historic Site)

봉황, 신산 꼭대기에서 바라보다

Bonghwang Gazing from the Summit of the Sacred Mountain

금성산에서 바라본 부여
Buyeo Viewed from Geumseongsan Mountain

Great Gilt-bronze Incense Burner of Baekje

Envisioning the Baekje People's Ideal World

Regarded as the very essence of Baekje culture, the Great Gilt-bronze Incense Burner of Baekje was brought to light on December 12, 1993. It was unearthed inside a wooden water tank at the workshop area of a temple site discovered in the locality of Neungsan-ri, to the west of the royal tomb complex in Buyeo, during an excavation conducted for the construction of a parking lot.

Based on the inscription on the stone reliquary (567, National Treasure) unearthed from the site of the wooden pagoda, the temple at Neungsan-ri is understood to have been established during the reign of King Wideok (r. 554–598) as a royal memorial temple (wonchal) dedicated to King Seong (r. 523–554), who fell in the Battle of Gwansanseong in 554. At the time of excavation, shards of roof tiles and layers of clay were found carefully stacked above the incense burner, suggesting that it may have been hastily concealed or protected when the capital city of Sabi fell in 660.

The incense burner measures 62.3 cm in height and weighs 11.8 kg. It consists of three parts: the lotus-shaped body, representing the world of immortals; the pedestal, formed as a dragon; and the lid, depicting a sacred mountain realm surmounted by the mythical creature *bonghwang*(phoenix). The lotus form of the body symbolizes creation myths in ancient civilizations as well as the pure and ideal realms of Buddhism. Resting upon the lotus petals is a lively assemblage of creatures—winged fish, human figures riding animals, waterfowl, otters, and other beings of the water, land, and sky—coexisting in harmony. Supporting both the body and the lid, the dragon pedestal rises in a powerful, dynamic posture that enhances the overall vitality of the work.

The lid represents the sacred mountain of the immortals, an ideal realm in Daoist thought. At its summit, a *bonghwang* gazes serenely downward, holding a pearl beneath its beak. Below it, five musicians are rendered in exquisite detail, as if performing celestial music with instruments such as the Baekje three-string lute, vertical flute, double-reed pipe, Baekje Zither, and drum. Flowing mountain ridges, human figures, animals, and mythical spirit creatures are arranged with remarkable sculptural skill, forming a narrative of beings traversing this utopian landscape. When incense smoke rises, this sculpted world creates the visual illusion of coming alive.

The Great Gilt-bronze Incense Burner of Baekje reinterprets the tradition of the Boshan-shaped incense burners of the Han dynasty China, integrating Baekje's distinctive sculptural sensibilities and religious worldview. While elements such as the *bonghwang* and mountain peaks reflect influences from the culture of the Northern and Southern dynasties, the presence of animals like elephants and monkeys—native to southern regions—suggests Baekje's interactions with areas of Southeast Asia. The iconography of the incense burner embodies a synthesis of Daoist immortality beliefs, indigenous spiritual traditions, and the widespread Buddhist faith, together reflecting the spiritual landscape of Baekje society.

The Great Gilt-bronze Incense Burner of Baekje is not merely a ritual vessel but a work that encapsulates the Baekje kingdom's conception of royal authority, its vision of a religious ideal world, and the pinnacle of its aesthetic achievement. It may be regarded as the apex of ancient East Asian metalwork and an iconic masterpiece symbolizing Baekje culture.

국보사진집

백제금동대향로 百濟金銅大香爐
부여扶餘에서 바라보다

기획	신영호 이정인
진행	이정인 이유라
원고 · 편집	이정인
향로설명	김왕국
사진촬영	한정엽(한국문화재사진연구소)
영문번역	장통방
디자인	장동석 최수현
인쇄제본	㈜두성프린트
초판발행	2025년 12월 19일
발행	국립부여박물관 33156 충청남도 부여군 부여읍 금성로 5 https://buyeo.museum.go.kr
출판	㈜디자인나눔 03780 서울특별시 서대문구 신촌역로 17 현대캠퍼빌 2층 http://designnanoom.com

Photo Album of National Treasures

Meeting the Gaze of Great Gilt-bronze Incense Burner of Baekje, Buyeo

Planning	Shin Youngho Lee Jungin
Coordination	Lee Jungin Lee Yura
Text & Editing	Lee Jungin
Photography	Han Jungyup(1971 Han Studio)
Commentary	Kim Wangguk
English Translation	Jangtongbang
Design	Chang Dongseok Choi Soohyun
Printing & Binding	Doosungprint
Date of Publication	December 19, 2025
Publisher	Buyeo National Museum 5 Geumseong-ro, Buyeo-eup, Buyeo-gun, Chungcheongnam-do 33156, Republic of Korea http://buyeo.museum.go.kr
Publication	Designnanoom 205 Hyundai Campaville, 17 Sinchonyeok-ro Seodaemun-gu, Seoul 03780, Republic of Korea http://designnanoom.com

ISBN 978-89-97595-71-6-93630
가격 34,000원

백제금동대향로
부여에서 바라보다
국립부여박물관